P9-DHK-629

GREEN BAY PACKERS · SUPER BOWL CHAMPIONS

I, JANUARY 15, 1967
35-10 VERSUS KANSAS CITY CHIEFS

II, JANUARY 14, 1968
33-14 VERSUS OAKLAND RAIDERS

XXXI, JANUARY 26, 1997
35-21 VERSUS NEW ENGLAND PATRIOTS

SUPER BOWL CHAMPIONS

GREEN BAY PACKERS

AARON FRISCH

CREATIVE EDUCATION

COVER: QUARTERBACK BRETT FAVRE

PAGE 2: THE PACKERS DEFENSE TACKLING A RUNNING BACK

RIGHT: WIDE RECEIVER ANTONIO FREEMAN CELEBRATING

Published by Creative Education
P.O. Box 227, Mankato, Minnesota 56002
Creative Education is an imprint of The Creative Company
www.thecreativecompany.us

Book and cover design by Blue Design (www.bluedes.com)
Art direction by Rita Marshall
Printed by Corporate Graphics in the United States of
America

Photographs by Dreamstime (Rosco), Getty Images (Lee
Balterman/Sports Illustrated, Vernon Biever/NFL, Matt
Campbell/AFP, Jonathan Daniel, Jonathan Daniel/Allsport,
David Drapkin, Andy Hayt, Al Messerschmidt, Darryl
Norenberg/NFL, Pro Football Hall of Fame/NFL, Frank
Rippon/NFL, John Zich/AFP)

Copyright © 2011 Creative Education
International copyright reserved in all countries. No part of
this book may be reproduced in any form without written
permission from the publisher.

Library of Congress Cataloging-in-Publication Data

Frisch, Aaron.
Green Bay Packers / by Aaron Frisch.
p. cm. — (Super Bowl champions)
Includes index.
Summary: An elementary look at the Green Bay Packers
professional football team, including its formation in 1919,
most memorable players, Super Bowl championships, and
stars of today.
ISBN 978-1-60818-018-9
1. Green Bay Packers (Football team)—History—Juvenile
literature. I. Title. II. Series.

GV956.G7F75 2011
796.332'640977561—dc22   2009053503

CPSIA: 040110 PO1141

First Edition
9 8 7 6 5 4 3 2 1

CONTENTS

6

Say It Like This

Lambeau:

LAM-boh

SUPER BOWL CHAMPIONS

Green Bay is a city in Wisconsin. Only about 100,000 people live in Green Bay. It can be very cold there. Green Bay has a **stadium** called Lambeau Field that is the home of a football team called the Packers.

PACKERS FACTS

First season:
1919

Conference/division:
National Football Conference, North Division

Super Bowl championships:
I, January 15, 1967 / 35-10 versus Kansas City Chiefs
II, January 14, 1968 / 33-14 versus Oakland Raiders
XXXI, January 26, 1997 / 35-21 versus New England
Patriots

Training camp location:
Green Bay, Wisconsin

NFL Web site for kids:
http://nflrush.com

The Packers are part of the National Football League (NFL). All the teams in the NFL try to win the Super Bowl to become world champions. The Packers' uniforms are green and gold. One of their main **rivals** is the Chicago Bears.

SUPER BOWL CHAMPIONS

The Packers played their first season in 1919. Curly Lambeau coached the team and played running back, too. He helped the Packers become NFL champions in 1929, 1930, and 1931.

... CURLY LAMBEAU (LEFT) AND PACKERS PLAYERS IN 1930 (RIGHT) ...

SUPER BOWL

In 1933, the Packers got a fast wide receiver named Don Hutson. He helped Green Bay win three more championships in 1936, 1939, and 1944. The Packers were not as good after that until they hired a smart coach named Vince Lombardi in 1959.

SUPER BOWL CHAMPIONS

Green Bay won the first two Super Bowls ever played, after the 1966 and 1967 seasons. Because the Packers had won so many championships (or titles), people called Green Bay "Titletown, U.S.A."

... DON HUTSON (LEFT) AND VINCE LOMBARDI (RIGHT) ...

Say It Like This

Favre:

FARV

It took a long time for the Packers to become champions again. In the 1990s, they had a new quarterback named Brett Favre. He helped Green Bay win Super Bowl XXXI (31) and then make the **playoffs** many more times.

SUPER BOWL CHAMPIONS

Say It Like This

Nitschke:

NITCH-kee

The Packers have had many stars. Clark Hinkle was a strong fullback who scored a lot of touchdowns. Linebacker Ray Nitschke led the Packers' defense in the 1960s with his rough tackles.

... RAY NITSCHKE PLAYED FOR THE PACKERS FOR 15 SEASONS ...

SUPER BOWL CHAMPIONS

17

SUPER BOWL CHAMPIONS

Bart Starr was the NFL's best quarterback in the 1960s. He threw **accurate** passes. Wide receiver Sterling Sharpe was another Packers star. He made the **Pro Bowl** five times.

The Packers added quarterback Aaron Rodgers in 2005. He threw 28 touchdown passes in his first season as a **starter**. Green Bay fans hoped that he would help lead the Packers to their fourth Super Bowl championship!

... AARON RODGERS LED THE PACKERS TO THE PLAYOFFS AFTER THE 2009 SEASON ...

WHY ARE THEY CALLED THE PACKERS?

When Green Bay's football team was formed, it got its uniforms and equipment from a meat-packing company. To show their thanks, the players called themselves the Packers.

GLOSSARY

accurate — on target, or thrown right where it needs to be

playoffs — games that the best teams play after a season to see who the champion will be

Pro Bowl — a special game after the season where only the NFL's best players get to play

rivals — teams that play extra hard against each other

stadium — a large building that has a sports field and many seats for fans

starter — someone who plays at the beginning of a game (not a backup)

23

INDEX